MARK

LECTIO DIVINA FOR YOUTH

MARK

LECTIO DIVINA FOR YOUTH

ANCIENT FAITH SERIES

Barefoot Ministries®
Kansas City, Missouri

Copyright 2007 by Barefoot Ministries®

ISBN 978-0-8341-5015-7

Printed in the United States of America

Written by Jim Moretz

Senior Editor: Bo Cassell
Editor: Mike Wonch
Assistant Editor: Jeremy Coleson
Cover Design: JR Caines
Interior Design: Sharon Page

Adapted from *Lectio Divina Bible Studies: Listening for God Through Mark*.

Moretz, Jim. *Lectio Divina Bible Studies: Listening for God Through Mark*. Indianapolis, IN: Wesleyan Publishing House and Beacon Hill Press of Kansas City, 2006.

Library of Congress Cataloging-in-Publication Data

Moretz, Jim.
   Listening for God through Mark / [written by Jim Moretz].
      p. cm. — (Ancient faith series)
    ISBN 978-0-8341-5015-7
   1. Bible. N.T. Mark—Devotional literature. 2. Bible. N.T. Mark—Textbooks. 3. Youth—Religious life. I. Title.

   BS2585.54.M67 2007
   226.3'00712—dc22

                                    2007013303

10 9 8 7 6 5 4 3 2 1

ABOUT THE
LECTIO DIVINA
BIBLE STUDIES

Lectio divina (pronounced lek-tsee-oh dih-vee-nuh), is a Latin phrase that means *sacred reading.* It is the ancient Christian practice of communicating with God through the reading and study of Scripture. Throughout history, great Christian leaders have used and adapted this ancient method of interpreting Scripture.

The idea behind *lectio divina* is to look at a Bible passage in such a way that Bible study becomes less about study and more about listening. The approach is designed to focus our attention on what God is saying to us through the Word. Through the process of *lectio divina* we not only read to understand with our minds, but we read to hear with our hearts and obey. It is a way of listening to God through His Word.

Some throughout history have said that *lectio divina* turns Bible study on its head—normally we read the Bible, but in *lectio divina, the Bible reads us.* That is probably a good way to describe it. It is God using His Word in a conversation with us to read into our lives and speak to our hearts.

In this series, we will use the traditional *lectio divina* model. We have expanded each component so that it can be used by both individuals and by groups. Each session in this study includes the following elements. (Latin words and their pronunciation are noted in parentheses.)

- **Reading** (*Lectio* "lek-tsee-oh"). We begin with a time of quieting ourselves prior to reading. Then we take a slow, careful reading of a passage of Scripture. We focus our minds on the central theme of the passage. When helpful, we read out loud or read the same passage over and over several times.
- **Meditation** (*Meditatio* "medi-tah-tsee-oh"). Next, we explore the meaning of the Bible passage. Here we dig deep to try to un-

derstand all of what God might be saying to us. We think on the passage. We explore the images, and pay attention to the emotions and feelings that the passage provides. We put ourselves in the story. We look for particular words or phrases that leap off the page as the Spirit begins to speak to us through the Word.

- **Prayer** (*Oratio* "or-ah-tsee-oh"). As we meditate on the passage, we respond to God by communicating with Him. We specifically ask God to speak to us through His Word. We begin to dialog with Him about what we have read. We express praise, thanksgiving, confession, or agreement to God. And we listen. We wait before Him in silence, allowing God the chance to speak.

- **Contemplation** (*Contemplatio* "con-tehm-plah-tsee-oh"). At this point in our conversation through the Word, we come to a place where we rest in the presence of God. Our study is now about receiving what He has said to us. Imagine two old friends who have just talked at length—and now without words, they just sit together and enjoy each other's presence. Having spent time listening to God, we know a little better how God is shaping the direction of our lives. Here there is a yielding of oneself to God's will. We resolve to act on the message of Scripture.

GROUP STUDY

This book is designed to be useful for both individual and group study. To use this in a group, you may take one of several approaches:

- **Individual Study/Group Review**. Make sure each member of the group has a copy of the book. Have them read through one section during the week. (They will work through the same passage or portions of it each day that week.) Then, when you meet together, review what thoughts, notes, and insights the members of the group experienced in their individual study. Use the group questions at the end of the section as a guide.

- **Group Lectio**. Make sure each member of the group has a copy of the book. Have them read through one section during the week in individual study. When you meet together as a group, you will study the passage together through a reading form similar to lectio divina:

- ○ **First, read the passage out loud several times to the group**. Group members respond by waiting in silence and letting God speak.
- ○ **Second, have the passage read aloud again to the group once or twice more**. Use different group members for different voices, and have them read slowly. Group members listen for a word or two that speaks to them, and share it with the group. Break into smaller groups if appropriate.
- ○ **Third, read the passage out loud again, and have the group pray together to ask God what He might be saying to each person, and to the group as a whole.** Go around and share what each person is learning from this process. At this point, review together the group questions at the end of the section.[1]

- • **Lectio Divina Steps for Groups**. Make sure each member has a copy of the book. As a group, move through the study together, going through each of the parts: reading, mediation, prayer, and contemplation. Be sure to use the group questions at the end of the section.

The important thing about using *lectio divina* in a group is to remember that this is to be incarnational ("in the flesh")—in other words, we begin to live out the Word in our community. We carry God's Word in us, (in the flesh, or incarnate in us) and we carry that Word into our group to be lived out among them.

The *Lectio Divina Bible Studies* invite readers to slow down, read Scripture, meditate upon it, and prayerfully respond to God's Word.

---

1. Parts of the "Group Lectio" section adapted from Tony Jones, *The Sacred Way: Spiritual Practices for Everyday Life*, Grand Rapids: Zondervan, 2005, p. 54.

CONTENTS

Introduction   11

Preparing the Way of the Lord   13

That We Might Be with Him   21

Accepting God on His Terms   29

Disregarding the Status Quo   37

Letting Go of Our Lives   45

The Christian Life Is Living for Others   53

The Strength of Worship   61

Living the Resurrected Life   69

INTRODUCTION

Have you ever read a great story? Whether it is fiction, non-fiction, history, or a biography, people enjoy a great story. Have you ever heard a story that changed your life? The Gospel you are about to study was written by Mark, or John Mark, as he was known. He was an associate of the disciple Peter. We know Peter was close to Mark because he refers to him as "my son Mark" (1 Peter 5:13). This Gospel was written by Mark, as told to him by Peter. In other words, Peter told the story to Mark and Mark wrote it down. However, this was no ordinary story. This was and is the story of Jesus' life and ministry. It is not just history, biography, or nonfiction; it is a story of one who came to change the lives of humankind.

According to scholars, this was the first Gospel story written and was circulated among the early followers of Christ. It was written while there were still living eyewitnesses to the life and ministry of Jesus who could corroborate the amazing events. The Gospel of Mark emphasizes such things as faith, repentance, the Cross, discipleship, and the teachings of Jesus.

The first words of this fast-paced account couldn't be more direct: "The beginning of the gospel about Jesus Christ, the Son of God." With these words, Mark sets the tone for the whole Gospel. This is the beginning story of One who came to change the world, especially for those who place their faith and trust in Christ. It is not just a story about a man, but is a story of the Son of God who came to die that we may live. The key to understanding the picture of Jesus shown in Mark's Gospel may be found in Jesus' own declaration, "For even the Son of Man did not come to be served, but to serve, and to give his life as a ransom for many" (Mark 10:45).

PREPARING THE WAY
OF THE LORD
LISTENING FOR GOD THROUGH MARK 1:1-20

SUMMARY

The Boy Scout motto is simply "Be Prepared." Preparation, it has been said, is the key to success in anything you really want to accomplish. So we prepare for everything from a test, term paper, and speech to a sporting event, band concert, and date. We build a solid foundation in the hope of achieving a good result. We prepare in order to have control—or at least influence—on what happens in the future.

We must also prepare ourselves for an encounter with Christ. In order to meet Christ, we must be prepared for His presence and calling upon our lives. It also means we avoid the temptation of trying to control our lives and its future.

Repentance (the act of confessing our sins to God and turning away from our life of sin), trust, and compassion are key elements in our preparation for meeting Jesus. When we follow Christ, our actions and their outcomes are under His control. That means we place ourselves in His hands. So getting ready to meet Jesus is not a matter of preparing to do something, but of preparing to be faithful to His call. This means being ready to do whatever He asks.

PREPARATION ☦ FOCUS YOUR THOUGHTS

God has promised to come to us. As you think about Christ's coming into *your* life, what is your reaction? Does your heart beat faster? Do you feel anxiety or excitement?

READING ☦ HEAR THE WORD

In his opening chapter, Mark prepares his readers to hear the story of Jesus. He does this by telling of the ministry of John the Baptist, who has been called the forerunner of Christ. (A forerunner is one who goes ahead of another person, letting people know that the person is coming and giving them time to prepare for that person.) John's ministry was rooted in the message of the prophets of the Old Testament, which points to the saving work of God through the coming Messiah (Jesus). In describing John, Mark combines the words of one Old Testament prophet, Isaiah, with the visual image of another, Elijah.

John called Jews to be baptized for the forgiveness of their sins. Jews regularly washed for ceremonial cleansing, but baptism was usually practiced only for Gentiles (non-Jews) who converted to Judaism. So John's call was a radical step, causing Jewish people to rethink their standing with God under the covenant (the agreement between God and His people).

Galilee was a surprising place for Jesus to begin His ministry. Jews from Galilee were the first to be exiled at the hands of the Babylonians several hundred years before the time of Christ, and inhabitants of the region had a reputation for unfaithfulness to the covenant. Galilee also had a significant Gentile population, and Jews in and around Jerusalem looked unfavorably at those from Galilee.

Read Mark 1:1-20 aloud, paying close attention to words or phrases that create a sense of urgency, making you want to read on.

MEDITATION ✝ ENGAGE THE WORD

Meditate on Mark 1:1-8

What do think about *repentance*? Do you find it inviting? challenging? unlikable? Why do you react as you do? Why do you think Mark begins his Gospel with a story about repentance?

Billy Graham says, "*Repentance means to change your way of living. It means to change your mind, you are going in one direction in your life, but then you turn and go in another direction.*"

How often do you think it is necessary to repent? Is repentance a one-time act, a continual process, or both? In what ways might a person's life change after repentance? What direction is your life going right now?

Mark says the Jews confessed their sins as they were baptized. What is confession?

> That evil spirit will no longer be able to vex you, nor will that foul serpent [Satan] henceforth make his lurking place in you, as he has been dragged out into the light from the darkness by your life-giving confession.
>
> —Abbot Serapion

Read the quote above. What does it mean that confession drags Satan into the light where he is exposed and condemned? Have you ever confessed a sin to someone else? How did you feel afterward? Did confession help in overcoming that sin? What is the relationship between confessing and repenting?

Meditate on Mark 1:9-13

Jesus was baptized by John the Baptist. This signified the beginning of His earthly ministry. This also signified His identification with the sinfulness of humanity and the acknowledgment by God as His Son and our Savior. Although He had never sinned, He identified himself with our sin. What lessons on the subject of sharing our faith might we get from this passage? What can you do to identify yourself with sinners, as Jesus did?

Read the quote below from George MacDonald. How does this statement relate to Jesus' command to "love your neighbor as yourself"? In what way is Jesus' baptism an example of that command?

> There is no feeling in a human heart which exists in that heart alone—which is not, in some form or degree, in every heart. —George MacDonald

Meditate on Mark 1:14-20

When we prepare to meet Jesus, we must be prepared to follow Him. He gives a simple call: "Come, follow me" (Mark 1:17). To that call, Jesus adds a promise: "Come, follow me, and I will make you fishers of men." There is no promise of success. Jesus promises only a purpose, a mission. As we follow Jesus, trusting Him totally, we see His path unfold before us. At first, however, we must decide whether we trust Him enough to follow Him.

Read the quote below from Mother Teresa. What have you dreamed of doing for God? When and how have you heard His call upon your heart and life? Were you afraid?

> *Let's do something beautiful for God.*
>
> —*Mother Teresa*

PRAYER ✞ ASK AND LISTEN

Seek the face of God. Ask, "Lord, what are you saying to us today?"

Confess and repent of your sins before God. Pray for the salvation of others. Ask God for the strength to follow Him wherever He leads.

CONTEMPLATION ✞ REFLECT AND YIELD

God has promised to come to us. Reaffirm your belief that He will come to you and ask you to follow Him.

What dream has God laid upon your heart? Do you trust Him enough to act upon that dream? Do you trust Jesus to make you who He wants you to be?

GROUP STUDY

- Why are some sins more difficult to confess and repent of than other sins?

- Why are confession and repentance important when it comes to following God?

- How do we recognize God's call on our lives?

- How hard is it to leave your comfort zone and follow God's call?

- Why is it difficult to trust God's plan, especially when we have no idea where it might lead?

- With a partner, discuss what you will do to act upon God's call on your life. Name the first action you will take this week on your journey with Jesus.

THAT WE MIGHT
BE WITH HIM
LISTENING FOR GOD THROUGH MARK 3:13-35

SUMMARY

Think about the people you like to be around. What you do and where you go do not matter; you just like hanging out with them. Jesus wants to be with us. Yes, He does have things to teach us and we must obey His commands. Yet, He chose His disciples that they might be with Him. Before Jesus sent the disciples into the world to heal the sick, cast out demons, and proclaim the good news, He spent time with them.

It is no different for us.

There may be days when the pressures of life seem to get all our attention and we are tempted to neglect spending time with Jesus; rather than focusing on the mission He has called us to. However, a disciple (a person who follows the teaching and example of another) represents the Teacher. In order to be like Jesus in the world, we must first have an intimate relationship with Him. He chose us so that we might be with Him.

Therefore our first challenge as disciples is to increase our sense of His presence. Jesus desires us to be with Him.

PREPARATION ✠ FOCUS YOUR THOUGHTS

Have you ever been specially picked for something? Maybe you were chosen to play on a sports team or were assigned a certain responsibility that only *you* could do. How did it feel to be chosen?

READING ✠ HEAR THE WORD

In Bible times, choosing a disciple was an important and intimate process. In essence, the teacher was selecting a person to be part of his family. Jesus designated 12 of His disciples as apostles. The word *apostle* means, "one who is sent." Jesus chose them in order to send them into the world bearing His name and His message. Becoming a follower of Jesus required total commitment.

Family heritage had a different implication in the time of Jesus than it does today. In Jesus' day, your family relationship determined your place in society. It is significant, then, that the choosing of Jesus' disciples is closely linked to Jesus' statement about His family: "Whoever does God's will is my brother and sister and mother" (v. 35). This means that membership in God's family is a matter of obedience, not birth. Jesus' words would have had a powerful effect on His Jewish hearers, who believed that their place in God's family was a matter of birth.

As you read this passage, hear it as Jesus' original audience must have heard it—as a radical call to abandon everything and follow Him.

Have one person in your group read aloud Mark 3:13-35.

MEDITATION ⚜ ENGAGE THE WORD

Meditate on Mark 3:13-19

In the Bible, mountains are symbols of authority. Mark emphasizes the authority of Jesus by telling us that He went up on a mountainside to call His disciples. Does Jesus have authority in your life? In what areas of your life do you find it difficult to allow others to have authority over you? Do you ever resist giving Jesus complete authority over your life? Why, or why not?

Read the quote on page 24 from the apostle Paul. Is it hard for you to believe that Jesus calls *you* to be His disciple? Could feelings of unworthiness get in the way of a person serving Jesus? How?

> *The saying is sure and worthy of full acceptance, that Christ Jesus came into the world to save sinners. And I am the foremost of sinners; but I received mercy for this reason, that in me, as the foremost, Jesus Christ might display his perfect patience for an example to those who were to believe in him for eternal life.*
>
> *—Paul (1 Tim. 1:15-26, RSV)*

It is probably no accident that Mark lists the apostles by name. Why? Jesus' call is a personal one. Have you ever thought about the fact that Jesus knows your name? Have you ever felt that He was calling you by name? How do you think it would feel to hear Jesus speak directly to you?

Meditate on Mark 3:20-22

After Jesus began His ministry, some members of His own family questioned His actions. Has anyone ever accused you of being weird or unwise for believing in Jesus? Have you ever been accused of doing something bad when you were actually doing something good? How did this make you feel?

Read Jesus' quote on page 25, and then read the quote from the Supertones below it. In what way might Christianity be considered "irrational"? Describe a time when your faithful actions may have appeared irrational.

> *If someone slaps you on one cheek, offer the other cheek also. If someone demands your coat, offer your shirt also.* —Jesus (Luke 6:29, NLT)
>
> *I'm a freak. They say I've lost my mind, but I know I've never seen more clearly. And when I speak, they say I've gone too far this time.* —The Supertones

Jesus' teaching and behavior caused Him to be seen as different from His culture and even His own family. Do you think others see you as being different because you are a follower of Christ? How so?

How can people tell you are a Christian?

Meditate on Mark 3:23-35

What does it mean to be a part of Jesus' family? What doubts did you have before you came to Jesus? How were they resolved?

Read Jesus' words on page 26. How does being with Jesus change your worldview? In what ways does your time spent with Him have an influence on how you view yourself?

> *Blessed are you when people insult you, persecute you and falsely say all kinds of evil against you because of me. Rejoice and be glad, because great is your reward in heaven.* —Jesus (Matt. 5:11-12)

How did Jesus respond to being misunderstood by His family? How do you respond when you are misunderstood as a follower of Christ?

PRAYER ✝ ASK AND LISTEN

Seek the face of God. Ask, "Lord, what are you saying to us today?"

Tell Jesus that you give Him total control of your life. Thank Him for calling you by name. Tell Jesus that you are willing to be set apart for His mission; then, rest in His presence.

CONTEMPLATION ✝ REFLECT AND YIELD

There is nothing more important for a Christian than to know Jesus. How well do you know Him? How much time do you spend with Him each day? Quietly listen for the voice of God. Allow God to say, "I chose you to be with Me."

GROUP STUDY

- What does it mean to you that Jesus calls you by name? How can you recognize His voice?

- What does it mean to be part of God's family?

- List several words that describe how you see yourself as a follower of Jesus Christ. Do you think other people see you in that way? Why, or why not?

- List the ways in which you, as a believer in Jesus, should be different from the world around you.

- Identify one thing you will do—or refrain from doing—this week that will remind you that you are set apart for a purpose.

ACCEPTING GOD ON HIS TERMS

LISTENING FOR GOD THROUGH MARK 4:10-34

SUMMARY

A popular fast-food restaurant used the saying, "Have it your way." That was many years ago. However, the statement has become a way of life for our society. We are so used to having things our own way that it is tempting to think of it as our right. In today's passage, we learn that the kingdom of God operates through higher standards. Here, size, strength, and status do not matter. We must enter God's kingdom on His terms. We must accept His gift as it is given to us.

God does not offer to make us taller, thinner, or more popular. He offers to make us like himself—holy, loving, and self-sacrificing. Yet, in order for that to happen, we must step out in faith. If we look for Him, we will see Him. If we listen, we will hear.

PREPARATION ⚜ FOCUS YOUR THOUGHTS

What is your most precious possession? Which of your possessions do you value most? Can a valuable possession be something intangible like education, freedom, or a relationship?

READING ⚜ HEAR THE WORD

Parables were a common way of teaching in Bible times. A parable is a brief story, usually centered on everyday activities, from which a lesson is taught. Many parables are told as riddles, and some are not easily understood. In Jesus' day, people would gather to hear a teacher just because his parables were difficult to understand, thinking the level of difficulty was a sign of the teacher's wisdom and knowledge.

Ancient teachers used hard-to-understand parables for two reasons. First, they wanted to determine which students were serious about studying. Second, they wanted to encourage students to wrestle with complex ideas. Ancient rabbinic sayings (related to rabbis and their teachings) held that God placed challenging content in the Scriptures to invite us to seek Him more.

In Mark's Gospel we see a difference between disciples, who were serious about following Jesus, and the crowds, who were mainly interested in Jesus' healing power. Those who wanted quick, easy answers remained on the outside. Being a true follower of Jesus required faith to step inside and believe in the Kingdom that Jesus talked about.

Silently read Mark 4:10-34, asking God to help you hear the meaning of these words.

MEDITATION ☦ Engage the Word

Meditate on Mark 4:10-20

Have you ever known anyone who claimed to be a follower of Jesus but didn't act like one? Is following Jesus a matter of faith, a matter of action, or both? Why, or why not?

Read the quote below from Dietrich Bonhoeffer. Have you ever taken a step of faith that has radically affected your whole existence? What led you to take that radical step?

In the Gospels the very first step a man must take is an act which radically affects his whole existence. Unless a definite step is demanded, the call vanishes into thin air, and if men imagine they can follow Jesus without taking this step, they are deluding themselves like fanatics. Discipleship is not an offer man makes to Christic. —Dietrich Bonhoeffer

What are the greatest sources of stress in your life? How does taking a definite step of faith have an influence on your attitude and response to those stresses?

Has your heart ever been so "hard" that God's Word could not take root? What caused this hardness? Did you overcome it? If so, how? If not, why?

Meditate on Mark 4:21-25

The statement "If anyone has ears to hear, let him hear" occurs both in this text and at the end of each of the letters to the seven churches in the Book of Revelation. What do you think Jesus meant by this statement? Think about the three words *anyone, ears,* and *hear.*

How do you react when you come across an idea that is difficult to understand? Do you think about it? Search for more information? Give up and move on? What is the reason you react the way you do?

What is your usual practice for reading or studying Scripture? What is the last message you received from God while reading the Bible? What are some of the ways you are able to effectively meditate on God's Word?

Read the quote below from Helmut Thielicke. Describe a time when a teaching from Scripture brought you to the point of leaping or retreating.

> If one examines the conversations of Jesus, one will note they always end in an arrest, in a sudden termination of the circular. Without exception they end in a "Hic Rhodus hic salta" (Here you must leap or retreat). They end at the steep escarpment of a message that cannot be avoided by any detour.
>
> —Helmut Thielicke

Describe a time when you carefully considered the meaning of a Bible passage and applied it to your life. How does the saying "Use it or lose it" apply to our use of Scripture? Give an example of how that might be true.

Consider the amount of energy you use reflecting on God's Word. Do you spend more or less time reflecting on other things such as music, school, or relationships, than you do on God's Word?

Meditate on Mark 4:26-34

What message do you get from the parable of the sower, the parable of the lamp on a stand, and the parable of the grow-

ing seed? How are the messages related? What does each one
tell us about our part in our relationship with God? What is
God's part in this relationship?

Read the quote below from Dietrich Bonhoeffer. What is the
difference between seeking to be good and seeking to know
God's will? How does that difference have an effect on your
relationship with God? How does that difference have an influence on your daily life?

> Whoever wishes to take up [Christianity] . . . must dis-
> card as irrelevant . . . two questions, "How can I be
> good?" and "How can I do good?" and instead of these
> he must ask the utterly and totally different question
> "What is the will of God?"   —Dietrich Bonhoeffer

PRAYER ♱ ASK AND LISTEN

Seek the face of God. Ask, "Lord, what are you saying to us
today?"

In the Garden of Gethsemane Jesus prayed, "Not my will, but
yours be done" (Luke 22:42). Pray those words. Then allow
God to speak to you, revealing His will for your life.

CONTEMPLATION ♱ REFLECT AND YIELD

God reveals himself to us in order that we can know Him. Be

silent in the expectation that God will reveal himself to you through His Word. Think about the ways in which you are trying to force God to do your will. Are you willing to accept God solely on His terms?

GROUP STUDY

- What does it mean to accept God on His terms?

- What are ways we try to force God to accept our terms?

- Name some of the ways in which we can be more open to God's leading.

- How does reading and meditating on God's Word allow God to speak to us?

- What is one thing God has revealed to you lately through His Word?

- Mark notes that Jesus explained many things to His disciples when He was alone with them. Name a time and place where you will be alone with Jesus each day this week.

DISREGARDING THE STATUS QUO
LISTENING FOR GOD THROUGH MARK 5:21-43

SUMMARY

Have you ever heard someone say, "That's just the way it is"? These words do little to ease the pain of those who are experiencing things such as illness (physical or mental), divorce, or abuse. People who are suffering need something more, they need hope.

People who suffer often feel bound to their suffering. They believe it is the life they have been dealt, so they must deal with it. C'*est la vie* (That's life), as the French say. Life is the way it is, and many people fear that it will never change.

Twice, Jesus ignored those who put forth this sort of world-view. Twice, those who believed in Him were shown another life. In these two stories from Mark, Jesus rejects "the way it is" and points to a better way. In Jesus, a better way exists—a way that leads to healing, hope, and eternal life.

Use this lesson to see through Jesus' eyes. A better way to live is around the corner.

PREPARATION ⚜ FOCUS YOUR THOUGHTS

Are there things in your life you would like to change, or are you content with life as it is? In what ways do you simply accept your circumstances? In what areas of your life do you need to experience a new perspective?

READING ⚜ HEAR THE WORD

Mark continually emphasizes that the power structures of the world are ultimately subject to the rule of Christ. Here he tied together two stories concerning women, which is significant considering women had very little status or power during Bible times. Jesus' teachings always have a radically different message from that of the culture.

In one story, a woman is considered unclean by society because of her chronic bleeding. Although she was viewed by others as cursed by God, the woman ignored social norms and touched Jesus. Jesus also ignored social expectations by responding to her. The woman trembled at His feet, fearing punishment for her actions; instead Jesus offered healing, forgiveness, and peace.

The other story describes the death of a synagogue official's daughter. In that culture sons were mourned far more than daughters, being seen as more productive and greater blessings. Daughters were viewed only as necessary. Yet, Mark shows this father, a powerful man, begging at the feet of Jesus for his little girl.

Mourning was very important in Bible times and the manner in which someone mourned was significant—the louder the mourning, the more important the person or family. A person could even hire professional mourners.

Read Mark 5:21-43 slowly, twice. Imagine yourself as a part of the crowd following Jesus, looking over heads and between shoulders to see what He will do next.

MEDITATION ⚜ ENGAGE THE WORD

Meditate on Mark 5:21-24

People pushed through large crowds regularly to get to Jesus. If you had lived back then, would you have reacted to Jesus in the same way? When have you had to ignore the opinions of others to get to Jesus? Have the opinions of others ever kept you from expressing your faith?

Read the quote on page 40 from Gustave Le Bon. How influenced are you by the crowd? What are some crowds in your life that you have to push through to get to Jesus?

> *In a crowd every sentiment and act is contagious and contagious to such a degree that an individual readily sacrifices his personal interest to the collective interest.*
> —Gustave Le Bon

Jairus went to Jesus because a major tragedy was about to occur; his daughter was dying. Do you wait until things have gotten bad before you seek God's help? Have you neglected to take the little things in your life to Jesus? How does seeking the Lord only when things go wrong limit your spiritual life?

Read Jesus' words below. What little things has God entrusted to you? How are you being faithful with them?

> *Whoever can be trusted with very little can also be trusted with much.*
> —Jesus (Luke 16:10)

Why is it important that we see God as the God of the little things? How does this help us ignore the crowds when we need to seek Jesus?

Mark simply says, "So Jesus went with him" (5:24). How does God's presence give us comfort when we are in the middle of the pushing crowd?

Meditate on Mark 5:25-34

Some people think that they do not need medical doctors, believing God will heal them if they are spiritual enough. Have you ever been praying for healing (physical or spiritual) and felt as if you were not spiritual enough to be healed? How much faith is required to be helped? Is there anyone Jesus will not help? Have we ever made anyone feel unworthy of Jesus' help?

We may know some answers to these questions, but, if we are sincere in them, how do they have an effect on our spiritual lives? Would we be more likely to reach our family, school, and community for Christ if we understood the implications of God's unbiased love?

How does it make you feel knowing that Jesus continued to look for the person who had touched Him even after the disciples told Him it was impossible to tell who it was?

Why did Jesus call the woman "daughter"? How does this connect the two stories Mark has tied together?

Meditate on Mark 5:35-43

It is easy to get discouraged if we have prayed about an issue for a long time without resolution, especially if the situation grows worse. The break in Jairus's story is helpful. Has there ever been a time when you prayed and still felt discouraged? Did those around you ever encourage you to give up? Did anyone encourage you to continue to seek God's help and guidance?

The key is overcoming fear. Jesus says, "Don't be afraid; just believe" (5:36).

Read the quote below from Pierre Teilhard de Chardin. What hopeless situation has the Lord brought you through? Have you ever had to simply trust in God, because it seemed as if there was no chance the situation would work out for you?

> We have only to believe. And the more threatening and irreducible reality appears, the more firmly and desperately must we believe.
>
> —Pierre Teilhard de Chardin

Is there someone in your life whom you want to become a follower of Jesus Christ, but whose commitment to Him seems unlikely? Do you think people would laugh at you if they knew you are praying for that person's salvation? How does this passage encourage you?

PRAYER ⚜ ASK AND LISTEN

Seek the face of God. Ask, "Lord, what are you saying to us today?"

The righteous walk by faith and not by sight. Pray for God to allow you to see your world through faith. Ask Him to help you overcome those fears that hinder your faith.

List all the little things in your life that God cares about. Thank Him for never giving up on you.

CONTEMPLATION ⚜ REFLECT AND YIELD

Psalm 46:10 says, "Be still, and know that I am God." Take a few moments to be still and acknowledge He is God.

Consider that "all things are possible with God" (Mark 10:27), and "I can do everything through [Christ] who gives me strength" (Phil. 4:13). Are there situations you have given up on? Are there people you have given up on?

GROUP STUDY

- What crowds are you pushing up against to get to Jesus?

- Can we become the crowd blocking others from Jesus? How?

- Do we sometimes require more of people than Jesus does? How?

- How can we be an encouragement to people when we hear them talk about how bad things are?

- Invite someone to church whom you do not think will ever come or needs the hope only Christ can give.

- Find little ways to serve in the Church and do them as if they are the most important tasks.

LETTING GO OF OUR LIVES

LISTENING FOR GOD THROUGH
MARK 8:31—9:13

SUMMARY

Surrendering our lives to Jesus is at the heart of Christianity. But what does it mean to *surrender our lives*? Does it mean we allow Him to *totally* direct our lives, or are there areas that we can still keep under our control? Giving your life to Jesus means being willing to abandon *all* that you think you know about this life in order to learn a new way of life.

The first principle is not to be afraid of defeat, or even death. In fact, following Jesus may result in temporary defeat, or death. Knowing defeat will come, and possibly death, why would we turn our lives over to Jesus? Total surrender happens only if we are convinced He will give us new life.

The problem is that most of us view new life the same as this life, just a little better. In reading this passage, we come to a better understanding of what it means to have new life, so that we may have confidence in letting go of our old lives. Only through surrender can we have the things of God in mind.

PREPARATION ⚜ FOCUS YOUR THOUGHTS

Paul often spoke of putting off the old self. What does it mean to put off the old self? Are you the kind of person that has trouble letting go?

READING ⚜ HEAR THE WORD

Jesus taught about His suffering and impending death immediately after the disciples proclaimed Him to be the Christ (8:27-30). This announcement from Jesus would have caught His disciples off-guard. The Jewish nation expected the Messiah to come as a great warrior and restore power to Israel. If Jesus were to be killed, how would He restore this power? How could He be the Messiah?

In verse 35, Jesus suggests that the way to truly live is to have no fear of death. This is the essence of new life—a life not subject to death. Crucifixion was the way of death that awaited Jesus. Death on a cross was a popular way of executing criminals in the Roman Empire. But, as we know, death did not have its final effect on Jesus. In truth, His resurrection ensures believers that death is defeated, and is no longer a threat to us. The world we live in is subject to death, and anything gained by the world is also subject to death. However, eternal life in heaven is the gift of God. This is faith: to believe in something, something the world does not and cannot produce.

The Transfiguration (the event in Mark 9:2-13 in which the glory of Jesus as God's Son and Messiah was shown) is a wonderful illustration of new life. It reveals that in Jesus rests all of the Law (Moses) and all of the prophets (Elijah), and that God has been promising new life from the very beginning. Exodus 24:12-18 and 34:29-35 provide some parallel stories of transfiguration.

Read Mark 8:31-38, then pause briefly to reflect on the Word. Reread Mark 8:31-38, but now read all of the way through 9:13.

MEDITATION ☦ ENGAGE THE WORD

Meditate on Mark 8:31-38

Jesus did not mean that Peter was actually Satan; rather that Peter was playing the role of Satan—the role of an enemy of God's will. Why do you think Peter took Jesus aside after He had talked about His suffering and death? Why do you think Jesus responded to Peter so harshly?

Read the quote on page 48 from Dietrich Bonhoeffer. For Jesus, "being Christ" meant sacrificing His life for others. Why did Peter attempt to stop Jesus from His mission? Is it possible for us to prevent Christ from fulfilling His mission in the world today? How?

> *Suffering and rejection are laid upon Jesus as a divine necessity, and every attempt to prevent it is the work of the devil, especially when it comes from his own disciples; for it is in fact an attempt to prevent Christ from being Christ.*   —Dietrich Bonhoeffer

Read this second Dietrich Bonhoeffer quote below. Do you think it is the Church who bears the suffering of the world as Christ's representatives? Are suffering and rejection still a necessary part of the Church as they were for Jesus?

> *But the Church knows that the world is still seeking for someone to bear its sufferings, and so, as it follows Christ, suffering becomes the Church's lot, too; and bearing it, it is borne up by Christ.*
> —Dietrich Bonhoeffer

What is the significance of Mark illustrating that Jesus called the crowds and His disciples together? What made the disciples different from the general crowd?

Read the quote below from Jesus. How would you answer these two questions?

> What good is it for a man to gain the whole world, yet forfeit his soul? Or what can a man give in exchange for his soul? —Jesus (Mark 8:36-37)

Meditate on Mark 9:1-13

In Mark 9:1, what do you think Jesus meant by "kingdom of God"? How might God's kingdom come with power?

Read the quote below from Paul. What is the connection between resurrection and suffering—life and death? What kind of power do we have through knowing Christ?

> I want to know Christ and the power of his resurrection and the fellowship of sharing in his sufferings. —Paul (Phil. 3:10)

Referring to Mark 9:2-4, what is the significance of Jesus' appearance changing in the presence of God? How does God's presence change us?

Peter wanted to build three shelters so that the presence of Elijah, Moses, and Jesus could reside within those shelters here on earth. Why was Peter's suggestion a bad idea? Why can't we put God's presence in a building?

How do the Law and the Prophets of the Old Testament point us to Jesus? Can our church activities and practices point us to the true mission of Christ? How can they distract us from His true mission?

Read the quote below from Exodus 19:9. Why do you think God often spoke through something physical like a dense cloud or burning bush? What are some ways God speaks to us today?

> The LORD said to Moses, "I am going to come to you in a dense cloud, so that the people will hear me speaking with you and will always put their trust in you."
>
> —Exodus 19:9

Why do you think Jesus told the disciples not to say anything about what they saw until after the Resurrection? As Peter, James, and John did, discuss what "rising from the dead" means. What does Jesus rising from the dead mean to you?

Have you ever experienced a spiritual "rising from the dead"? How has this changed your life?

PRAYER ✝ ASK AND LISTEN

Seek the face of God. Ask, "Lord, what are you saying to us today?"

Close your eyes and breathe deeply. Anticipate God showing you a new life. Seek the Lord and ask Him to reveal to you areas in your life that you have not fully surrendered to Him. Pray that God will surround you with new life.

CONTEMPLATION ✝ REFLECT AND YIELD

Does the idea of Christ's resurrection have an influence on your day-to-day activities and decision-making? Has accepting this new life that Christ offers been a struggle for you? Do you easily slip back into your old way of life?

Since knowing Christ, how has your view of suffering changed? What are ways you find joy during times of suffering?

GROUP STUDY

- What are some ways people might experience suffering as a result of their faith in Christ?

- How do we experience God's presence in our lives?

- What are some ways that God can do something new in our lives, something we have never experienced?

- Is your new life radically different or merely the same as your old life?

- What changes can you make in your life this week to more fully experience new life in Christ?

- Write a paragraph about how your life has been changed by Christ.

THE CHRISTIAN LIFE IS LIVING FOR OTHERS
LISTENING FOR GOD THROUGH MARK 9:33-50

SUMMARY

It is part of human nature to want things our way. We want our voice to be heard. However, when we come to Christ and become His followers, our rights change. In Christ we learn that it is our right to help others before we help ourselves. We learn how to give and receive grace in relationships. We learn the Christlike way to relate to others. We learn the true meaning of service. This is the first lesson of Mark 9:33-50.

Also, in this passage, we learn to be honest about our own sinfulness. Jesus understands how we are likely to lower the seriousness of our sin, making ourselves not look so bad. His teaching gives us the ability to identify our sin and the courage and strength to avoid it. Nothing on earth compares to the peace and wholeness of living rightly before the Lord. Jesus changes our worldview, bringing the kingdom of heaven into focus while dimming the lights of the kingdom of this world.

PREPARATION ✝ FOCUS YOUR THOUGHTS

"If anyone wants to be first, he must be the very last, and the servant of all" (9:35). How can you serve others by putting them before yourself?

READING ✝ HEAR THE WORD

Jesus was, and is, the Master Teacher. During Bible times, a teacher sat down to teach as a sign of authority, so when Jesus sat down to teach His disciples, He assumed His rightful position of authority. Jesus then reorganized the concept of authority by using a child as His example. Children were not highly regarded in society until they could be a productive part of the community. Important people did not take time to deal with children. Yet, Jesus was trying to show that God desires for us to welcome children and learn from their innocence.

The ways of the kingdom of God are higher than our ways. The kingdom of God stretches us and challenges our preconceived ideas, as Jesus often did with His disciples.

In verses 42-50, Jesus uses hyperbole (a deliberate and obvious exaggeration used for effect) in His teaching of sin. He doesn't mean for us to actually gouge our eyes out. The use of hyperbole was a common teaching method in the time of Jesus. Jesus used this method to show that sin is deadly and should be removed at all cost.

Read Mark 9:33-50 aloud. Allow the Holy Spirit to point you to a word or phrase from the text. Repeat that word or phrase quietly.

MEDITATION ✟ Engage the Word

Meditate on Mark 9:33-37

Jesus knew what the disciples were arguing about, yet He asked them anyway. Why do you think He did this?

Read the quote below by Matthew Arnold. What is "the service of an ideal higher than that of an ordinary man" that Arnold spoke of?

> *Nations are not truly great solely because the individuals composing them are numerous, free, and active; but they are great when these numbers, this freedom, and this activity are employed in the service of an ideal higher than that of an ordinary man, taken by himself.*
> —Matthew Arnold

For Jesus, that *ideal* involves serving others, being the least among your peers, and caring for children. What does it mean for you?

In contrast to how those around you measure greatness, how does Jesus measure greatness? How do you measure success? Do you spend more time trying to achieve the world's ideal of greatness or God's?

In what ways are you serving others? Do you look for opportunities to serve?

God identifies with the poor, the abused, and the oppressed to the point that He became poor, abused, and oppressed. When we welcome others into our lives, we welcome God himself. How often are you and your church welcoming God?

Meditate on Mark 9:38-41

John worried that the man casting out demons in Jesus' name had not been authorized to do so. Jesus, however, was not concerned. In fact, the man's willingness to use Jesus' name affirmed his actions as being from God. Is it wrong to question someone who acts in the name of the Lord?

Read the quote on page 57 from John Milton. Doctrines are teachings that are agreed upon and accepted by people in a religious group. Christian doctrines are certain beliefs about God, the Bible and so on that are agreed upon and accepted by Christians. Doctrines are necessary, but how can they be an obstacle in the Church?

> *Though all the winds of doctrine were let loose to play*
> *upon the earth, so Truth be in the field, we do injuri-*
> *ously, by licensing and prohibiting, to misdoubt her*
> *strength. Let her and Falsehood grapple; who ever*
> *knew Truth put to the worse, in a free and open en-*
> *counter?* —John Milton

Can spending time defending our own doctrines prevent us from serving others? How can the defense of doctrines have an effect on the Church and the mutual work of all believers?

Meditate on Mark 9:42-50

Verses 33-37 illustrate the incorrect way to view oneself (as great). Verses 38-41 illustrate the incorrect way to view other believers (mandating that they be like you). How does verse 42 correct these two mistaken points of view?

Read the quote below from Walt Whitman. What would a child become if he or she followed your example? Are their changes you need to make in your actions?

> *There was a child went forth every day,*
> *And the first object he look'd upon,*
> *that object he became.*
> —Walt Whitman

Looking at sin as a virus, how does your sin affect others? How can sin be contagious?

Study the progression in the last four verses of the passage. Verses 47-48 remind us that, while dealing honestly with sin can cause pain, it is nothing compared to the pain of eternal separation from God. Jesus' statement in verse 49 assures us that everything will eventually be shown for what it is. There is no use in hiding sin, therefore we repent (confess and turn from our sin) and receive forgiveness.

What connection do you see between verse 50 and verses 33-34?

Read the Carl Jung quote below. In which shadow do you rest, love or power? Would your church be characterized as a church of love or a church of power? How does the authority we have in Jesus relate to the issue of power?

> *Where love rules, there is no will to power; and where power predominates, there love is lacking. The one is the shadow of the other.* —Carl Jung

PRAYER ⚜ ASK AND LISTEN

Seek the face of God. Ask, "Lord, what are you saying to us today?"

Spend three minutes in silence listening for the voice of God. Listen as a child listens for his or her mother and father. Leave everything at the feet of Jesus.

Ask God to reveal any hidden sins in your life. Pray that He will give you a willing spirit to serve others.

CONTEMPLATION ⚜ REFLECT AND YIELD

The Church is a collection, a congregation, of servants. Are you an active member of the Body of Christ? The Christian faith is comprised of many denominations. Are you quick to serve fellow Christians or judge their differences? How open are you to learning about how Christians outside of your church practice Christianity?

GROUP STUDY

- How can we become more like a child in our faith?

- What are ways we can welcome others into our lives?

- How can we be more open to other Christians, denominations, and churches without losing and compromising our own held beliefs?

- What are ways we can serve God in our home? school? community?

- Name one way you can be a "salty" example to someone younger than you.

- Think about your upcoming week. In what ways can you live the life of a humble servant?

THE STRENGTH OF
WORSHIP
LISTENING FOR GOD THROUGH MARK 14:18-42

SUMMARY

We all need strength to live the Christian life in a fallen world. Disappointment, fear, and weakness trouble our existence. The answer to these threats and the source of our strength lie in worship. Worship helps us recognize our own inabilities and reliance upon God's ability. Jesus said the spirit is willing, but the flesh is weak (Mark 14:38). In the Garden of Gethsemane, Jesus was troubled by the disciples' lack of strength, warning them to watch and pray that they might not fall into temptation.

On the eve of His crucifixion, Jesus demonstrated how strength is gained through worship. Praying early in the morning was Jesus' custom, recorded often in the Gospels, and here we see Him seeking His Father with gut-wrenching passion. The institution of Holy Communion, the singing of hymns, and prayer are also seen in this passage as wonderful forms of worship. Understanding the strength worship provides will increase your excitement for worship and ultimately revolutionize your life.

PREPARATION ⚜ FOCUS YOUR THOUGHTS

How do you personally gain strength through worship? In your most difficult moments, are you drawn to the Church, to prayer, or do you have a tendency to withdraw?

Consider your favorite parts of worship, and praise God for His creativity and diversity.

READING ⚜ HEAR THE WORD

The Last Supper which Jesus and His disciples shared together was a Passover Seder, an official Jewish meal memorializing the time when the Angel of Death passed over the Hebrew houses that had lamb's blood sprinkled on the doorway.

Some interesting differences exist between the actual Passover recorded in Exodus 12:1-30 and the Feast referred to in this passage. The first Passover meal was eaten fast, with staff in hand, ready to go at God's call. Later Jewish feasts, by contrast, required reclining at the table, so as not to rush the meal and neglect the meaning. Another difference is that Mark makes no mention of Jesus and the disciples eating the lamb, which was the centerpiece of the meal in Exodus. This may be Mark's hint to the reader that Jesus is the Passover Lamb of the new covenant.

The Passover feast was a time of celebration; however, while they were eating and reclining at the table, Jesus dulled the mood by saying that one of them would betray Him. In the midst of celebrating God's faithfulness, Jesus was betrayed by one who was eating with Him.

Read Mark 14:18-42 slowly, several times. Don't be in a hurry, but allow God's Word to fill your mind.

MEDITATION ☦ ENGAGE THE WORD

Meditate on Mark 14:18-26
This section can be further divided into 18-21, 22-25, and 26.

Read the quote below from E. M. Forster. What is Forster saying about the importance of relationships?

> If I had to choose between betraying my country and betraying my friend, I hope I should have the guts to betray my country.   —E. M. Forster

How does worship keep our focus on people and relationships?

What is the significance of Jesus' body and blood? What are we celebrating when we take Communion? Read the quote below from Paul. When we take Communion, how do we proclaim "the Lord's death"? How often do you celebrate Holy Communion? How does it give you strength?

> For whenever you eat this bread and drink this cup, you proclaim the Lord's death until he comes.
>
> —Paul (1 Corinthians 11:26)

What hymns or worship choruses do you like? Have you ever thought about why you like them? Do their words ever come to your mind during the week?

Meditate on Mark 14:27-31

Peter's story of denial is another example of how the spirit is willing but the body is weak. Have you ever experienced this?

Describe something you have tried to do on your own but failed. What could you have done differently?

Later, Peter denies Jesus three times. What made Peter think, at this point, that he wouldn't? Read the quote on page 65 from the apostle Paul. How do his words relate to this story?

> For what I want to do I do not do, but what I hate I
> do. . . . What a wretched man I am! Who will rescue me
> from this body of death? Thanks be to God—through
> Jesus Christ our Lord!   —Paul (Rom. 7:15, 24-25)

We worship on Sunday in celebration of the day of the Resurrection. How should this influence our approach to worship? Would worship be possible without the Resurrection? Why, or why not?

Jesus saves us in spite of ourselves and our sin. Knowing this truth, how does it influence your worship? Do you stand humbly before God?

Meditate on Mark 14:32-42

What does night represent in this passage? In the Gospel of John, Jesus is called "the light" (John 1:4). Notice the contrast of the Light praying in the darkness.

Read the John 1:4-5 passage below. How do these verses from John have an effect on your reading of this passage in Mark?

> In him was life, and the life was the light of men. The
> light shines in the darkness, and the darkness has not
> overcome it.   —John 1:4-5, RSV

How personal is Jesus' relationship with the Father? How personal is your relationship with Jesus? How does the level of your relationship with Jesus have an influence on your prayers?

Have you ever been broken in prayer? Describe what the experience was like.

Read the Henry Vaughan poem below. Night has both negative and positive implications. We all need rest, but when does rest become an obstacle to our spiritual growth? What feelings does "night" bring up for you?

> *Dear Night! This world's defeat;*
> *The stop to busy fools; care's check and curb;*
> *The day of spirits; my soul's calm retreat*
> *Which none disturb!*
> *Christ's progress, and His prayer-time;*
> *The hours to which high*
> *Heaven doth chime.*
>
> —Henry Vaughan

What does Jesus mean by "Watch and pray so that you will not fall into temptation" (14:38)? How determined are you to "pray through the night"—that is, to pray through your trials and troubles? Do you give up too easily?

PRAYER ✟ ASK AND LISTEN

Seek the face of God. Ask, "Lord, what are you saying to us today?"

When Brother Lawrence made a mistake or committed a sin, he would pray something like, "Without You, O Lord, that would be my whole life." Pray for an understanding of worship as a source of strength for your life.

CONTEMPLATION ✟ REFLECT AND YIELD

"Recline at the table" before God and prepare to feast on His Word. Slow your breathing as you relax in the presence of the Almighty God.

Do you approach worship with the expectation of receiving grace from God? How can you be more intentional in your worship?

GROUP STUDY

- What comes to mind when you think of worship?

- What are the different ways we can worship God?

- How is Communion a part of worship?

- How do we worship God with our words and actions?

- How can we make worship become more meaningful?

- How can worship be a source of strength for us?

- For the next two weeks, keep a paragraph journal about how your worship gives you strength. Include your private prayer times and devotionals along with your public worship. Find a partner or group who will join you in this exercise, so that you can share your experiences with each other.

LIVING THE
RESURRECTED LIFE
LISTENING FOR GOD THROUGH MARK 16:1-20

Summary

Jesus referenced His coming resurrection often to His disciples, yet when they received the good news, they did not initially believe it. Their motives were pure, not wanting to be fooled, but, as the saying goes, "The road to hell is paved with good intentions."

The same may be true of us. Most of us have heard of the resurrection of Jesus. Yet how many of us truly believe it? Many Christians have good motives. They work hard, avoid the bad, and try to do the good. However, believing in the Resurrection requires risk; we must go beyond what we think is normal or good living and embrace the radical pronouncement of the angel messenger in Mark 16:6: "You are looking for Jesus the Nazarene, who was crucified. He has risen! He is not here."

We must also follow Jesus back to where it all began, back to the origin of sin; but this time we have the victory. We walk through sin's territory as a conquering army, defeating Satan's forces and freeing those he has captured.

PREPARATION ☦ FOCUS YOUR THOUGHTS

At first, the story of the Resurrection may seem like a fairy-tale. Have you ever struggled with believing this unbelievable story? What happened when you fully understood the truth of the Resurrection?

READING ☦ HEAR THE WORD

The first chapter of Mark begins with the baptism of Jesus. The last chapter leads us to His tomb. There we find Mary Magdalene, Mary the mother of James, and Salome. They brought spices to anoint the body of Jesus. In Bible times they did not embalm (place fluids in the body to prevent decay); instead oils were normally applied to the body. However, these women brought spices in order to show their love for Jesus. This meant two things: they came to honor Jesus, and they did not expect Him to have risen from the dead. They thought He was still in the tomb. Thus their question, "Who will roll the stone away?"

However, when they arrived, the stone was rolled away and the tomb was empty. All that was there was a "young man dressed in a white robe." Verse 5 says "they were alarmed." Who wouldn't be? You get to the tomb, the stone is rolled away, Jesus' body is gone, and there is a strange man sitting inside. Again, they were afraid. Who wouldn't be?

In their state of fear the angel told them not to be afraid. Why? Because "Jesus the Nazarene, who was crucified. He has risen!" The angel told the women to go and tell the disciples and Peter. He is risen! This was great news then, and is GREAT NEWS to us today. He is RISEN!

The NIV and most contemporary translations contain the statement "The earliest manuscripts and some other ancient witnesses do not have Mark 16:9-20." Besides this lack of textual evidence, some features within the passage suggest that it was added later, and possibly not by Mark. Regardless, a faithful reading should lead us to greater understanding of the resurrection of Jesus.

Read Mark 16:1-20 aloud, even if you are alone.

MEDITATION ⚜ ENGAGE THE WORD

Meditate on Mark 16:1-8

The women came to finish the burial ritual, which was cut short by the Sabbath. However, they were worried about rolling the huge stone away from the tomb entrance. What "huge stones" in your life are in the way of serving Jesus? What does the Resurrection mean for those stones?

Read the quote below from Arthur Schopenhauer. Are you looking at the world through your limited scope of vision or through the wide lens of the Resurrection?

> *Every man takes the limits of his own field of vision for the limits of the world.* —Arthur Schopenhauer

The women walking to the tomb that morning did not see what they expected to see. How has God surprised you recently? How did you react?

Most people fear change, even change that is good. We can become so used to our difficulties that trusting God's guidance and direction is more frightening than our current situation. How does the Resurrection ease our fears about God's call on our lives?

The women feared no one would believe them. Are you afraid to tell others what God is doing in your life?

Meditate on Mark 16:9-14

What is the significance of Jesus appearing first to Mary Magdalene? What does the fact that Jesus had driven seven

LIVING THE RESURRECTED LIFE

demons from her add to her story? What implications does this have in regard to your relationship with Jesus?

When Mary saw Jesus, her fear disappeared, and she went and told the others what she saw. How does fear influence the way you share your faith?

Read the Schopenhauer quote below. How does this analogy have an effect on your desire to reach out and invite others to be a part of the Church?

> *Every parting gives a foretaste of death; every coming together again a foretaste of the resurrection.*
> —Arthur Schopenhauer

By appearing to His disciples and then sending them out to others, Jesus created the Church, a gathering of those who believe in the Resurrection.

73

Meditate on Mark 16:15-20

Read the quote below from Romans 10. The "good news" is that death has been defeated. How does this make you feel? Do you have the "beautiful feet" Paul is talking about? If not, how can you get them?

> How, then, can they call on the one they have not be-lieved in? And how can they believe in the one of whom they have not heard? And how can they hear without someone preaching to them? And how can they preach unless they are sent? As it is written, "How beautiful are the feet of those who bring good news!"
>
> —Paul (Rom. 10:14-15)

Does Mark 16:16 give you a sense of urgency?

Read the quote below from Paul. How can you interpret the signs Jesus gives in Mark 16:17-18 in light of Paul's words? Some of the signs are hard to understand, but how can we use them to understand living the resurrected life? How bold-ly should we proclaim the gospel?

> If God is for us, who can be against us?
>
> —Paul (Rom. 8:31)

Jesus' resurrection means victory. How positive should we be about the victory we have in Jesus, not only over our own sins, but over the world and its sin? What does that victory mean to our mission to spread the gospel?

Read the quote below from Martin Luther. Why is the Resurrection central to the Christian faith? How can you make it central in your life?

> The leading thought, however, for us to learn and retain from this Gospel is, that we believe that Christ's resurrection is sure and that it works in us so that we be resurrected from both sin and death.
>
> —Martin Luther

PRAYER ♱ ASK AND LISTEN

Seek the face of God. Ask, "Lord, what are you saying to us today?"

Pray for God to give you a deeper understanding of the Resurrection and how your life can reflect its truth. Pray for your church that it would celebrate the Resurrection and share the message with your community.

CONTEMPLATION ☦ REFLECT AND YIELD

Imagine the intense sadness you would have felt that Sabbath morning, after being a companion of Jesus for three years, as He lay lifeless in the tomb. Then imagine seeing Him alive again! Silently reflect on the joy of the Resurrection.

Are you living for God with everything you have? Is the gospel radical in your life? Do you carry with you the positive sense that sin and death have been defeated? Are you watching for opportunities to tell others about the Resurrection?

GROUP STUDY

- Why is belief in the Resurrection crucial to our faith?

- The women who visited the tomb were told to tell others about the Resurrection. How can we share the good news that Jesus is risen?

- Do you struggle with fear when it comes to sharing your faith with others? Discuss your fears and doubts with a close friend or your small group.

- What actions can you take today to fully embrace living the resurrected life?

- Think of three people in your life with whom you can share your story as a witness to God's redeeming love. What are some benefits of sharing your story with them? What are some obstacles you may face?

- Mark tells the story about the life and ministry of Jesus. What difference has this story made in your life? How can you share this story with others?